COOL CAREERS WITHOUT COLLEGE FOR

PEOPLE

WHO LOVE

TO DRIVE

COOL CAREERS WITHOUT COLLEGE FOR
PEOPLE
WHO LOVE
TO DRIVE

ROBERT GREENBERGER

The Rosen Publishing Group, Inc.
New York

Published in 2004 by The Rosen Publishing Group, Inc.
29 East 21st Street, New York, NY 10010

Library of Congress Cataloging-in-Publication Data

Greenberger, Robert.
Cool Careers without college for people who love to drive / by Robert
Greenberger.— 1st ed.
     p. cm. — (Cool careers without college)
Summary: Explores the job descriptions, education and training
requirements, salary, and outlook predictions for twelve careers that
focus on driving and do not require a college education.
Includes bibliographical references and index.
ISBN 0-8239-3786-0 (lib. bdg.)
1. Motor vehicle driving—Vocational guidance—Juvenile literature.
[1. Motor vehicle driving—Vocational guidance. 2. Vocational
guidance.] I. Title. II. Series.
TL152.5 .G733 2003
629.28'3'023—dc21

                                                          2002007466

Manufactured in the United States of America

CONTENTS

INTRODUCTION

One of the greatest days of your school career has nothing to do with classes. It has everything to do with getting your driver's license. With it comes the freedom to get around on your own. No longer do you have to wait for someone else to be available to drive you. Your days of being embarrassed to ride with Mom or Dad are over. Freedom isn't the only thing you'll gain. Learning to drive might also open up more than a few career opportunities.

If you love driving, then you might want to consider one of the occupations surveyed in this book. For some people, just the act of driving is cool enough. If that's the case, you might want to work as a messenger, sanitation driver, or taxi driver. On the other hand, if you crave the open road and want the chance to see more of your country, then you might want to consider truck driving or bus driving.

This book offers you a glimpse into twelve driving-related careers. Each entry includes information that will help you consider whether the career is for you, such as licensing and training requirements, job duties and lifestyle, salary and benefits, and the predicted future for the career. For almost all these jobs, you will need a commercial driver's license (CDL) in addition to your regular license. Additional training is usually called for, both in the classroom and on the road. It's important to keep in mind that each of the fifty states has different requirements, so it's always best to check with your state's department of motor vehicles to make sure you have the most current requirements.

Each chapter will refer you to books and Web sites for additional information, but for a general overview, check out the U.S. Department of Transportation's careers Web site at http://dothr.ost.dot.gov/Careers/main_c.htm. It has a lot of good general information and links.

When considering a career, it is always a good idea to talk to people in the line of work that interests you. Ask the men and women who drive for a living in your town and hear firsthand what they like and dislike about their work. You might discover that something that sounds glamorous turns out to be not at all what you want to do.

Most of these careers are expected to either remain stable or grow in the coming years. So if you like to drive, and the open road calls you, then by all means read on.

1

BUS DRIVER

If you like the thought of being responsible for getting a lot of people where they need to go, then driving a bus may be the job for you. The majority of opportunities for bus drivers are for school bus drivers. After all, just about every school district in America requires at least some students to be transported to and from school. But drivers are also needed for commercial outfits and private coaches chartered by groups. And, of course, there are also the city bus drivers who get people around town.

School bus drivers begin their day by checking over their vehicle to make sure it's ready to handle the students. They also are responsible for keeping the bus clean, oiled, and full of gas, in addition to immediately reporting problems that might prevent the bus from operating efficiently.

In addition to the regular routes around neighborhoods to and from school, school bus drivers will be hired to take students on field trips and teams to athletic meets. Drivers not only have to follow the routes but must maintain discipline in each bus. This means knowing the codes of conduct unique to each school district. Should something go wrong, the bus driver might be asked to administer first aid or help a physically disabled student.

City bus drivers have scheduled routes that they need to master quickly. Once they have passed the course work and are approved to drive, they generally start work as a substitute driver or handle extra routes added during peak seasons. When an opportunity opens, they are among those first considered for an opening. Driving a city bus can be fun because you may get to know your regular riders, but it can also be stressful for those who get aggravated by city traffic and gridlock.

A school bus driver watches as students board the vehicle. School bus drivers must monitor the behavior of the students on the bus without being distracted from driving safely.

Charter bus drivers get to hit the open road for short day trips and longer, overnight excursions. While the thought of long-distance driving may be appealing, please note that charter drivers tend to work the longest hours. Federal guidelines mandate that bus drivers drive no more than sixty hours in a seven-day period or no more than ten hours without being immediately followed by eight hours of rest. As a charter bus driver, you will drive on weekends and holidays, and your day will be dictated by the schedule of the bus company or the specific charter.

Requirements

In most cases, you need to be at least eighteen to drive a bus, but once you cross state lines, you will be subject to federal law. Federal law requires you to be at least twenty-one. City bus companies tend to look for people with some bus experience and a minimum age of twenty-four.

Federal law requires that you possess a commercial driver's license (CDL). The CDL test requires you to not only know how to drive but how to inspect your vehicle. For example, you will need to know how to check the hydraulic brakes, and you will need to know how to operate a clutch. Just like the exam for the regular license, the CDL test covers physical and driving regulations. For example, if you don't maintain a gap that allows you to see the rear bumper of the vehicle ahead of you, you will fail.

Those who commit driving offenses are added to the federal databank, which holds records of all infractions or suspensions. Being listed in the databank will prevent you from being licensed in any other state.

There are specific driving schools for larger vehicles like buses and trucks. Before you can be tested for your CDL, you will be asked to take a four-week course. A driver with a CDL will be working alongside you as you train, until you pass the test and get your own license.

Bus drivers are expected to assist passengers who need help getting on or off the bus, such as the disabled and the elderly.

Federal law sets standards for hearing and vision, and those who are color-blind may not receive a CDL. As a bus driver, you will be subject to physical exams every two years. Additionally, drivers must have free use of their arms and legs and maintain a stable blood pressure. There are also restrictions for people who suffer from epilepsy or diabetics who take insulin. Federal law further mandates that drivers must have a good enough command of the English language to follow maps, understand road signs, and communicate effectively with passengers.

Finally, drivers must pass a written examination on the U.S. Department of Transportation's Motor Carrier Safety Regulations.

Since they are being asked to ferry children as young as four or five to school, school bus drivers may be subject to background checks by cautious states. They may even be asked to submit to psychological exams.

City bus drivers must take special training, which covers the handling of schedules, operating the fare collection boxes and making change, and dealing with the general public. This training usually takes eight weeks to complete. States usually have additional testing for CDL candidates to make sure they can follow the complex route and time schedules required.

While all of this sounds like a lot to get through, think about all the people who have driven you around over the years. They all had to go through the same exams and passed, successfully handling buses for years. To enjoy this job, you must like to drive, not mind sitting still for hours at a stretch, and be willing to deal with people of all ages and temperaments.

Salary

Wages for school bus drivers tend to be set by school district contract, but the median wage according to 2000 statistics was $10.67 per hour. City and rural bus drivers tend to have contracts, and the 2000 median wage was $12.36 per hour. City drivers tend to earn more than those in rural

A Greyhound bus driver collects a passenger's ticket at the Port Authority Bus Terminal in New York City.

areas. Charter drivers are at the bottom of the scale, with a 2000 median wage of $10.27 per hour.

Depending upon the job, bus drivers will likely be protected by some type of union. School drivers in many states are covered by state employee guidelines that entitle them to sick leave and participation in the employee pension system. Benefits for city drivers tend to include sick and vacation leave and participation with a union such as the Amalgamated Transit Union. Coach drivers belong to the United Transportation Union or the International Brotherhood of Teamsters, which help establish benefits such as sick and vacation leave.

Outlook

There were 666,000 bus drivers in 2000, and the number is expected to grow at an annual rate of 1.7 percent through 2008, according to the Department of Labor. That number will change depending upon the region of the country. Texas, for example, is expecting a 13 percent annual increase in bus driving jobs through 2005. Given that the majority of driving jobs are for schools, over one-third of the positions are part-time, under forty hours a week. Two-thirds of the bus drivers in 2000 worked for school systems, while the remaining third worked in other roles.

FOR MORE INFORMATION

ASSOCIATIONS
American Bus Association
110 New York Avenue NW
Suite 1050
Washington, DC 20005
(202) 842-1645
Web site: http://www.buses.org
A professional organization that lobbies on behalf of drivers, seeking improved laws and safety rules.

American Public Transportation Association
1666 K Street NW
Suite 1100
Washington, DC 20006
(202) 496-4800
Web site: http://www.apta.com
An organization that lobbies on behalf of drivers, seeking improved laws and safety rules.

National School Transportation Association
P.O. Box 2639
Springfield, VA 22152
Web site: http://www.schooltrans.com
An organization that lobbies on behalf of drivers, seeking improved laws and safety rules with an emphasis on school issues.

United Motorcoach Association
113 South West Street
4th Floor
Alexandria, VA 22314
(800) 424-8262
Web site: http://www.uma.org
An organization that lobbies for all coach drivers, including charter, public transportation, and school buses.

BOOKS

Byrenes, Mike. *Barron's How to Prepare for the CDL: Commercial Driver's License Bus Driver's Test.*Hauppauge, NY: Barrons, 1991.

Calvin, Robert M. *Bus Driver's Guide to Commercial Driver Licensing: What You Need to Know to Become Licensed.* New York: Hungry Minds, Inc., 1990.

Research & Education Association. *CDL: Commercial Driver License Exam.* New York: R&EA, 1998.

Snyder, Robert W., and Pete Hamill. *Transit Talk: New York's Bus and Subway Workers Tell Their Stories.* New Brunswick, NJ: Rutgers University Press, 1997.
A nonfiction collection of first-person accounts of the horrors and humor of their jobs.

PERIODICALS

School Bus Fleet
21061 South Western Avenue
Torrance, CA 90501
Web site: http://www.schoolbusfleet.com/home.cfm
A print and online magazine for professional school bus drivers, complete with articles, editorials, and tips.

2

CHAUFFEUR

OK, you don't like large crowds, but you still like driving people around. Consider working as a chauffeur. When most of us think of chauffeurs, we imagine a mysterious gentleman dressed in a black suit and cap, driving a millionaire to his country club. Actually, most chauffeurs today aren't employed by private citizens, and they don't need to dress quite as formally.

Many chauffeurs work for high-profile clients such as business executives, politicians, and celebrities. These clients expect chauffeurs to not disclose any sensitive information they may overhear.

You still need to be presentable, clean and neat, and usually in a jacket and tie if you're a man. After all, you are representing a company or an image the paying passenger may want to convey to a business client or even a date. Drivers will be regularly asked to take people to work or home from a late night at the office. You may be asked to take a couple to the prom, a bride to her wedding, or a family to their grandmother's funeral. In some cases, you may work for one wealthy individual or family, staying on call and shuttling members wherever they need to go.

Your day starts with checking your vehicle to make sure not only that it is in good working condition but that it is shiny, neat, and in order. This may mean stocking it with a variety of drinks, newspapers, and magazines.

When collecting your passengers, you will be expected to greet them at the door, help them load their belongings, and assist them in entering and exiting the vehicle. They will determine what radio station, if any, is to be played and may give you favored routes to a destination. You will need to remain cheerful and even-tempered even if you disagree with a choice or dislike a selection.

In some cases, you will find yourself playing tour guide for someone who is new to the area. As a result, you need to be familiar with popular attractions such as zoos, museums, sporting teams, restaurants, and theater. You may be asked to make recommendations, so your base of knowledge needs to be broad and deep.

You will have to have a little business experience because you will need to know how to handle the billing as required by your company. This means you need to handle paperwork such as credit card receipts, or make change for those companies that still operate with cash. At the end of

Many couples hire chauffeured limousines to add a touch of luxury to their wedding.

each shift, you will report your trips and earnings back to your company, keeping the tips for yourself.

As a chauffeur, you will have the potential to meet fascinating people. If you make a good impression, you may be asked for by name in the future. Many drivers end up meeting celebrities at some point in their careers. On the East and West Coasts, drivers are sometimes hired to ferry stars to events or back and forth to movie or television sets. Your job future depends on your ability to be personable and discreet whether the passenger is a rock star or an exhausted businessperson. If a person wants to chat, you need to keep up your end of the conversation. If a person prefers not to have a conversation, you need to maintain silence. At all times, the passenger sets the tone for the trip. And each trip is different, which has a special appeal all its own.

Requirements

In addition to your regular driver's license, you will need a special license, commonly called a "hack's license," which allows you to drive for commercial purposes. In most cases, earning this license will require around eighty hours of

A chauffeur holds an umbrella over his boss's head. In addition to driving and helping clients in and out of the car, many chauffeurs perform numerous errands for their clients.

classroom instruction. The ability to read a map is essential. You'll need to know the major highways in the area. You must also know how to get around traffic snarls since most passengers are on some kind of schedule. You will also be expected to know how to handle basic first aid and how to help those with special needs. English proficiency will also be tested since you will need to know how to read road signs and communicate effectively with your passengers.

Many chauffeur companies tend to set minimum age requirements for their drivers that are higher than the age needed to get a driver's license. This varies from company to company. Their standards are higher than the state's since they need to project as professional an image as possible to attract clients. No one wants to be driven around by someone who doesn't appear to be able to handle difficult situations, should they arise.

Salary

Drivers are generally paid an hourly wage or commission per trip in addition to tips from passengers. As a result, it's difficult to determine exact incomes. However, the government estimates the median income for limo drivers to be $8.58 an hour. Self-employed drivers earn between $25,000 and $50,000 per year. Some companies work on a lease basis where drivers lease the vehicle from them for a set fee.

Drivers then set their rates and keep whatever they earn after the fee is paid off. Most drivers work long shifts, which are not subject to federal regulations. In many cases, this means ten- to twelve-hour days or longer, with the day starting in the wee hours of the morning or lasting well past midnight. You need to remain alert and professional at all times.

Outlook

There is a lot of turnover in this profession, which creates many opportunities for drivers. It also allows drivers a chance to grow within a particular company if they wish to get off the road and move into the office. According to government statistics, there were 176,000 people working as taxi or limousine drivers in 2000. About one-third of those drivers worked for suburban transportation or cab companies. The remainder did other forms of driving. A mere 27 percent of the drivers were self-employed.

Profile

Interview with Jack Sullivan, owner, Fairfield Executive Limousine in Connecticut.

WHAT DO YOU LOOK FOR IN A DRIVER?
In order of importance, I look for good work ethics. Next is presentability. You have to have a good personality. My

drivers have to be able to carry on a conversation with the person in the backseat. Then, experience. Has the person been to [local] airports, how long has he been driving? Finally, appearance.

WHAT TYPE OF DRIVERS DO YOU USE?

I have twenty-one vehicles with six full-time drivers. The rest of my drivers are part-time, and if I get busy, I bring in sub-contractors. I have a lot of young guys; but I also have guys who have lost their jobs in the middle of their career. I have two full-timers who are in their fifties and sixties, people who took early retirement.

TELL ME ABOUT SUB-CONTRACTORS.

These are people who own their own vehicles. I might have thirty jobs in a day and need them to fill out the schedule. They worry about maintaining the car, gassing it up, the insurance, and all the stuff I worry about with my own cars. They get paid on a per-job basis, and if they work for two or three companies, they can make a fine living this way.

WHAT ABOUT YOUR OWN DRIVERS?

They get paid per trip plus tips. My full-time drivers normally do three trips in a day. I would say they gross [pay before taxes] $670 to $840 per week.

IS THIS A GOOD CAREER TO PURSUE TODAY?

It's more of a step, not a career. I have drivers who solicit work from people in the back, although you have to feel

out the situation. Many passengers don't want to be bothered. It's a good opportunity for networking. Most of my drivers are doing this until they find something else. I only have two who see this as their career.

FOR MORE INFORMATION

ASSOCIATIONS

Canadian Taxicab Association
455 Coventry Road
Ottawa, ON K1K 2C5
Canada
(613) 746-8740
Web site: http://www.cantaxi.ca/calgary_conference.htm
A trade association for the private passenger industry in Canada. Like its American counterpart, it lobbies on behalf of companies and drivers.

National Limousine Association
49 South Maple Avenue
Marlton, NJ 08053
(800) 652-7007
Web Site: http://www.limo.org
An industry organization to help provide current information to limousine owners and operators.

Taxi, Limousine, and Paratransit Association
3849 Farragut Avenue
Kensington, MD 20895
(301) 946-5701
Web site: http://www.tlpa.org
A trade association for the private passenger industry, it has members from around the world, sharing tips and information and lobbying for laws that protect drivers and passengers.

BOOKS

Bromley, Michael L., and Tom Mazza. *Stretching It: The Story of the Limousine.* Washington, DC: Society of Automotive Engineers, 2002.
A technical look at the making of these vehicles, including the classy stretch variety.

Holly, Lou. *How to Succeed in the Limousine Business*. New York: All Charter Books, 2001.
A how-to guide for those with an entrepreneurial spirit.

Nyborg, Randall. *How to Start and Operate a Limousine Service.* Oldenburg, Germany: University Publishing House, 1992.
Another how-to guide for those with an entrepreneurial spirit.

PERIODICALS

Limousine & Chauffeured Transportation
21061 South Western Avenue
Torrance, CA 90501
(310) 533-2400
Web site: http://www.lctmag.com
A magazine and Web site specializing in the issues that affect drivers, passengers, and companies. Also has an e-mail newsletter.

3

COURIER/ MESSENGER

For people who like driving but don't necessarily want to be surrounded by passengers all day, an alternative might be working as a messenger, also known as a courier. Couriers drive around an area, usually a city or collection of towns, picking up and delivering packages. In cities, messengers

A bike messenger weaves his way through busy city traffic. Bicycle couriers are likely to be found in large urban centers where traffic gridlock is commonplace.

are as likely to ride a bicycle as drive a car, and they have their own culture.

In most cases, messengers work part-time, allowing them to attend school, raise a family, or look for other work. As a result, there remains high turnover, which creates frequent job opportunities.

Some messengers use the position as a chance to learn about the business and rise through the ranks. While this is a possibility, it is not common. Additionally, with the advent of e-mail, video conferencing, overnight express services, and fax, this is not expected to be a career growth area.

Some companies specialize in delivering different kinds of material, which may require you to learn how to handle all kinds of packages. For example, if you deliver medical samples, you will have to learn to handle sensitive packages containing blood or even organs. Documents, on the other hand, need a different kind of handling.

Most often you will be ferrying envelopes of all sizes from one location to another. These can be sensitive legal documents, bank information, letters, printed samples, and other seemingly routine items. While they may appear routine to you, it's vital to remember these are important to both sender and receiver, so treating the material carefully and with respect is a must. There will be times when you will be asked to handle boxes or heavy packages. As a result, you not only need to be in good physical shape, you need to make sure you have the right tools to do your job. This might mean a hand truck or cart in the back of your vehicle. Like the vehicle itself, these will need to be maintained in good working order.

You will also be responsible for getting the company's documents signed, completing a record that a package was picked up at a certain time and delivered at a certain time. This way, should the recipient claim not to have the package, there is a written record to track the delivery. These

records are also used for billing purposes, which will be handled by people at the office, not the driver.

Working as a messenger is important work that places a fair amount of responsibility on the driver, and can be a good way to get yourself noticed as you decide on a career.

Requirements

As a courier, you might be asked to drive a company vehicle or your own car. If you use your car, then all you need is a valid driver's license. In Canada, you need to be twenty-one years old to work as a messenger. If you drive a company-owned vehicle, you might be required to obtain a commercial license based on state guidelines. Typical job ads ask for people who already know a specific city or region. There is usually no training offered regarding routes or vehicle maintenance. Instead, you learn by doing, or in this case, driving.

Most couriers work for companies and are assigned vehicles. It will be your responsibility to keep the car, truck, or van clean, oiled, and full of gas. Most often, you will receive instructions via cell phone or two-way radio, and you will need to know how to operate the specific system.

A courier watches as the package's recipient signs the courier's delivery log. Being able to prove delivery of a package is almost as important as delivering it.

And even though timeliness counts, speeding does not, and you will be expected to maintain a clean driving record both on duty and off duty.

Salary

Messengers tend to work standard shifts, most likely with some overtime offered. You will be paid an hourly wage, and usually there is no tipping in making deliveries. For those at the upper end of the scale, it is not out of the question to earn upwards of $1,000 a week, but that will be obtainable for only a small percentage of drivers, and usually these jobs are located in major cities like New York and Los Angeles.

The median wage for a courier in 1997 was $8.01 per hour. Those handling medical material tended to earn the most, and those delivering basic envelopes and packages were at the bottom of the scale.

Outlook

Federal records show that there were about 120,000 people working as couriers in 1998. Some 14 percent of messengers worked directly for law firms, another 13 percent worked in the medical profession, and another 13 percent worked for trucking concerns. Financial institutions, such as commercial banks, savings institutions, and credit unions, employed 7 percent. The rest were employed in a variety of other industries, including general delivery services.

Profile

Charles Chiusano, president, Service Messenger, Manhattan's oldest messenger company.

WHAT DO YOU LOOK FOR IN A MESSENGER?

The messenger must be well presented, regardless of age. When he goes to a customer to make a pickup, he is representing our company. When he goes to make a delivery, he is then representing the customer. The driver must be clean-cut, which we reinforce with work rules. A person cannot do his or her job wearing a walkman-style device, for example.

The driver has to have a relatively good command of the language. English could be the person's second language, but he or she has to be able

Car couriers are more likely to deliver large, bulky packages.

to report to us or take information without asking for it to be repeated.

We'll do a background check, but not an especially deep one. We'll do that if the person works at a customer's mailroom, since we also provide mailroom personnel for companies.

WHAT'S THE MESSENGER'S DAY LIKE?

They work a ten-hour shift, five days a week. We pay them a commission based on the work completed. Some will volunteer to be on call nights and weekends, and since we charge higher rates then, they get more money.

All our messengers are owner/operators with their own vehicle. Most drive vans; others drive hatchback cars. They must insure the vehicle and maintain it, which we check occasionally. We provide them signage that they display. We also require that they buy and wear a uniform with our company logo on it. They also are required to wear a laminated photo ID on a chain around their necks. That's become increasingly important with heightened building security.

They keep in touch using a two-way radio, usually staying on the road the entire shift. The drivers have to worry about parking tickets, even with their commercial plates. And driving in Manhattan can be especially difficult.

Our messengers who hustle can earn $750 per week before expenses, so they can make a nice living at this.

IS THERE A LOT OF TURNOVER?

It's relatively low, actually. We have had many drivers with us for twelve years or more and some who last a year or year and a half. Some leave to start their own business or move out of the area.

WHAT ABOUT CAREER ADVANCEMENT INTO THE OFFICE OPERATION?

Honestly, it would be a pay cut to most and it's not done that often.

FOR FURTHER INFORMATION

ASSOCIATIONS

There are no lobbying organizations for couriers, but they may be eligible to join some of the other driver-oriented associations listed throughout this book. Please check each one.

WEB SITES

U.S. Department of Transportation's Career Page
http://dothr.ost.dot.gov/Careers/main_c.htm

BOOKS

Bruce, William H. *Secret Messengers: How Governments Correspond.* College Park, MD: Bruce Publishing International, Inc., 1995.
A look at the diplomatic courier and his or her environment.

4

DELIVERY DRIVER

Deliveries are made every day in your town. You probably don't realize just how many vehicles pass you by on their way to provide someone with a good or service. A delivery vehicle drops off the morning newspaper at your home; another brings oil or natural gas to keep you warm; at night your take-out dinner is brought by a delivery driver. In between, dozens of other delivery drivers crisscross every town and city in America doing their jobs.

These jobs are a cross between messenger drivers and truck drivers. Like messenger drivers, delivery drivers must know a specific region and manage to get deliveries to their destinations in a timely and safe manner. Like truck drivers, delivery drivers have to not only drive but likely load and unload the vehicle, which could contain anything from a lightweight pizza box to heavy furniture.

Requirements

As with most of the jobs in this book, you will need a commercial driver's license, depending upon the size and weight of your vehicle. Depending upon the type of delivery being made, you may need a partner or two to get the job done. Most times, though, the deliveries are made on your own. This is the type of job that requires a little more expertise than a messenger has, since you may need to know how to operate the delivery vehicle and all its functions. For example, if you deliver oil, you need to understand how the pump works, how to find the intake pipe at your destination, and how to safely deliver the oil.

Many deliveries are made in company-owned vehicles. This includes deliveries for overnight package services or regional dairies. In these cases, you will be operating a

A truck driver transporting gasoline prepares to complete a delivery by connecting her truck to a gas station's underground tank.

light truck, van, or panel truck. These are closer to a car in handling than larger trucks or specialized vehicles. You will need to have a CDL in most cases and will be obligated to follow the Department of Transportation's guidelines. Each state has its own specific guidelines as well, and you should consult your local state's department of transportation for details.

Delivery drivers usually report to a distribution center to pick up their cargo and their vehicle. In most cases, you will

Help Wanted

A typical ad for a company delivery driver reads as follows: "Clean-cut delivery drivers needed. Local delivery only. CDL license is NOT REQUIRED, but applicants are encouraged to apply. Must have clean driving record and knowledge of the area. Will be meeting with clients on daily basis so neat appearance is required. Must have no felonies in the past 7 years and a clean motor vehicle record [MVR], and must agree to a D.O.T. drug screen prior to hiring. Skills/Requirements: Clean MVR and valid driver's license, neat professional appearance, knowledge of area. Pay comments: depending on experience. Job status: full-time."

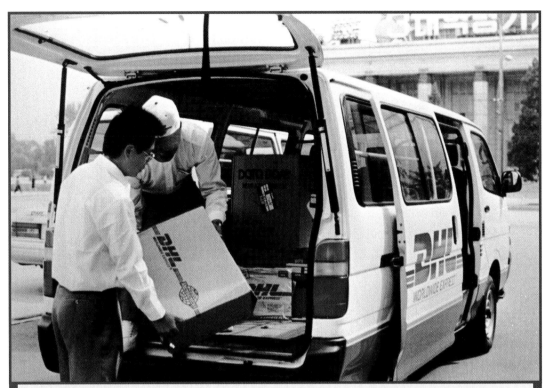

Delivery drivers need to know their way around their specific routes to ensure that they deliver a large volume of packages to the right destinations in a timely manner.

wear some form of identifying uniform, such as a shirt or jacket so people recognize that you represent a specific company.

For those who do not want to use another vehicle and prefer their own car, there are less specialized delivery jobs, such as pizza delivery. In these cases, you do not need a special license, but a clean driving record will be important. You will also need a knowledge of the vicinity, which will be more limited than, say, an overnight package company.

A national pizza chain advertises for drivers by pointing out, "Our driver position is an excellent start to learn about the delivery business, customer service, and the creation of a great product—from start to finish. [We're] committed to promotion from within—most of our managers started as drivers. It is a stepping-stone to advancement into our management development program. Even if you choose a different career path, you will learn skills for life!"

It should be noted that there really isn't room to move up, and this may be seen as a first job, not a career. On the other hand, note that President Harry S. Truman began his working life as a deliveryman.

Some companies prefer experienced drivers and look for them to be older than eighteen. In Toronto, for example, companies look for drivers who are at least twenty-two.

If you want to get started, this is perhaps the easiest entry field for a high school graduate and exposes you to different companies and work environments, which makes choosing your next career step much easier.

Salary

There remain too many types of delivery drivers to accurately gauge earning potential, but most of these jobs are full-time and pay hourly rates normally determined by region. Expertise comes into play as well, but you may find yourself earning under $10 an hour to start. Those who deliver items that require payment, such as take-out food, can expect closer to the minimum wage with tips supplementing the salary. Naturally, someone delivering oil is paid a higher hourly wage than someone dropping off dry cleaning.

Outlook

Given how many different delivery jobs exist, and that they are all hourly jobs, there is a reasonable amount of turnover in the delivery business. If you prefer the solitary drive, the familiarity of a single region, and the added responsibility, then this may be the driving career for you.

FOR FURTHER INFORMATION

ASSOCIATIONS

Most delivery drivers do not benefit from lobbying organizations, but they may be eligible to join some of the other driver-oriented associations listed throughout this book. Please check each one.

5

DRIVING SCHOOL INSTRUCTOR

Most everyone needs to learn how to drive, and most learn from an experienced instructor. Driving instructor is one of the more specialized careers for those who like to drive, given the specific skills it requires. Chief among those skills is patience, since driving instructors spend every day dealing with people who are just beginning to operate vehicles.

A driving instructor monitors the performance of a student driver.

To do this job well, you need to like people and have an ability to effectively communicate with them. Your personality has to be engaging so that the student receives the lesson in a positive manner. Remember your own experiences learning from an instructor? Or your parents? What would you do differently if you were to become an instructor?

As a driving instructor, you will be called upon not only to get in the car with students but also to give them the necessary classroom instruction. For many drivers, this is the first time they are given a thorough understanding of how a car works. They're taught what each part of the vehicle does and what to do should a part of the car fail to operate properly. They are usually taught basic safety instructions regarding what to do should they break down on a street or highway. Some instructors will teach how to properly change a tire in case of a flat.

Safety is perhaps the most important element stressed in class. Students are usually shown a film or video of car accidents, demonstrating what was done right or wrong and how to prevent accidents from occurring. As an instructor, you need to make sure the message gets through to your students.

On the road, you will generally be working in a driving-school vehicle outfitted with a special braking device on the front passenger side of the car. This dual brake gives the instructor the chance to stop the car should the driver make a serious error. It's there as a fail-safe device to protect student, instructor, any passengers, and pedestrians.

You will need to carefully show the driver how to park, make three-point turns, use the rearview and sideview mirrors, change lanes, operate a car on a highway, and so on. You will normally have about thirty classroom hours, in addition to eight to ten hours of actual driving time, with each student. This gives you thirty-eight hours to teach lessons that students will use for the rest of their lives. Therefore, this is an extremely important profession and should not be entered into lightly.

If you like the idea of teaching as a profession, be aware that your students may not be limited to beginning drivers. Certain models of cars earn a huge amount of devotion, and people form clubs around them. These clubs hire driving instructors to help them learn how to get the best performance from the cars.

You could also become a specialist in a particular area, such as racing, and work with professional drivers. Many race car drivers, when they choose to stop racing, become instructors for the next generation of drivers. Similarly, stunt drivers also open schools to teach people.

Requirements

Interestingly, given how vital this career is, there is no federal monitoring of instructors or guidelines about what needs to be taught. Instead, this falls to states to determine, and as a result there are at least fifty different approaches to the position. In Texas, for example, a would-be instructor needs to take a thirty-six-hour course. In Florida, it's just thirty-two hours.

Many driving schools in America offer courses to prepare future instructors. To find one, you will need to check your

Car racing instructors act as coaches and work on racing strategies with their clients.

Driving instructors sometimes double as driving education examiners or as judges at driving competitions.

local yellow pages. Professional driving instructors can work for independent companies or regional or national chains.

Future instructors are taught to have professional conduct and a clean driving record. States charge about $75 for an instructor's license. Make sure that the school you attend is a member of the Driver School Association of America, since they set the standards. In addition, the school should be accredited by the state department of motor vehicles. Most states require the instructor to be at least twenty-five years old for insurance purposes.

Salary

Driving instructors usually earn in the range of $15 per hour or per driving session. Most driving schools are privately owned so the salary ranges differ from region to region. Instructors who take students out on the road are generally paid per session regardless of time involved (going to and from the student's location plus lesson time). These can pay as high as $18 per class.

Outlook

The number of people who need to learn to drive will not diminish, so this should be a safe profession to enter into. Many insurance carriers offer lower rates to their customers who have logged hours with a driving instructor.

FOR FURTHER INFORMATION

ASSOCIATIONS

Driving School Association of the Americas
8511 West Lincoln Avenue
West Allis, WI 53227
(800) 270-3722
Web site: http://www.thedsaa.org
An international association representing Germany, Canada, Japan,

England, and the United States. It provides information regarding changes to state and federal laws and provides a forum where instructors can share information. Membership perks include group insurance benefits.

Driving School Association of Ontario
111 – 557 Dixon Road
Toronto, ON M9W 6K1
Canada
(416) 247-2278
Web site: http://www.dsao.com
This nonprofit organization is dedicated to maintaining and improving the professional standards of driver education in Ontario.

WEB SITES
Drivers.com
http://drivers.com
A comprehensive Web site for drivers of all kinds. Articles, links, and other information are available. A recommended site regardless of professional interest.

Manual of Traffic Signs
http://members.aol.com/rcmoeur/signman.html
A must-visit site for potential teachers. This site displays the most commonly used traffic signs you are likely to encounter while teaching your students.

6

STUNT DRIVER

More and more you see tiny type during car advertisements on television that reads "Professional driver." What does that mean? In most instances, it means the driver has been specially trained to handle a vehicle in all conditions for the purpose of entertaining. These drivers do the high-speed chases seen in movies and on television. They also

A stunt driver's car reaching speeds of 93 miles per hour sails 314 feet, setting a world record with this jump.

entertain the crowds at amusement parks, county fairs, and car shows. If you think that was really Vin Diesel driving in *The Fast and the Furious*, think again. He just had close-ups filmed while a professional handled the tricky driving.

All of these drivers have been to school and have trained long and hard to make the driving seem authentically reckless. Stunt driving looks cool, but it is the most dangerous driving discussed in this book. It is not for the faint-of-heart, nor is it for people who dislike taking risks.

This profession is strictly for those people who like to mix speed and skill with more than a little risk-taking.

The organization Stunts Canada best describes the job: "Stunt performing is its own unique craft. No skill you have will make you a good stunt performer, yet every skill you have will be useful in performing stunts. Just as rock climbing does not make you a good motocrosser, gymnastics does not make you a good stunt performer. Strive to learn everything you can, listen more than you talk, be very, very patient and if you follow the basics (learn the language of film [working as an extra], be diligent in your physical training, promote yourself as a stunt performer), and if you have a true passion for film, you can be successful as a stunt performer. It's the greatest job in the world."

Stunt performers sometimes work live as well, entertaining at monster truck shows or NASCAR events. Many stunt drivers shuttle between film work and live performance work. Mark Hager, for example, has coordinated stunts for and performed in hundreds of shows. In 1995, he broke a record by jumping 213 feet over a row of buses at NASCAR's Charlotte Motor Speedway Race. (Hager is from a family of stuntmen, which is not at all unusual in this profession.)

Stunt drivers usually maintain professional Web sites listing their accomplishments and featuring video clips of their best work. If you wish to become a stunt driver, you will have to assemble such a "clip reel" for prospective

Stunt drivers often perform spectacular crashes in movies. In this scene from *Ripperman*, a car crashes into a delivery truck loaded with bottled water.

employers. That becomes your résumé and calling card for any job that requires a professional driver.

Of all the careers surveyed in this book, this one may be the hardest to achieve. It may be even harder to sustain.

Requirements

There are many schools that teach race and stunt driving, but the best known is perhaps Bobby Ore's Motion Picture Stunt Driving School in California. It's a two-day program, as most are, and should be seen as the beginning of a long road toward making it in this profession. You need to log many hours of practice time, and you will be charged hourly fees to attain access to the closed courses. Ore writes on his Web site, "Any stunt performer will tell you that it is a constant training and learning process."

Once you gain the confidence required to be a stunt driver, you will then need to find people willing to work with novices. Television commercials may be the easiest access to this business, and commercial coordinators are the people to approach. Since most filmmaking is done in the Los Angeles area, it would be wise to relocate there so you can be closer to the opportunities. L.A.'s mild climate also allows you year-round access to driving courses. When you're not working, you can sharpen your skills.

To be considered for such work, you will need to join the Screen Actors Guild (SAG). The guild has strict rules about membership. This means you will first need to get some work in order to build up your credits so that you will be eligible to join the union. Once there, you will find resources to direct you to additional opportunities. Additionally, SAG works with state governments to ensure that whatever stunts are performed do not violate the law. The driver's safety is of the utmost concern, and if the driver does not feel the stunt called for is safe, he or she can refuse to perform.

Stunt driving is exciting but dangerous work, and requires nerves of steel. In this scene from the movie *Dark Breed*, two cars explode after crashing through a tractor-trailer rig that was pulling a mobile home.

Salary

Stunt drivers are paid for the work that is required for a particular job, so the rates are entirely flexible and negotiable. The greater the risk, the more money paid. But if you're a stunt driver on a film that involves a lot of car work, you stand to make more money given the time involved.

Outlook

The odds of finding work as a stunt driver are against you. It has been estimated by SAG that there are 5,000 stunt drivers out there, with maybe 250 working at any one time. How do those lucky few get the jobs? They are either in the right place at the right time, specialize in a particular stunt, or physically match the actor or actress playing the role that requires a stunt driver.

Stunt drivers have a limited life span in terms of career because sooner or later their reflexes start to slow them down. In some cases, a lifetime of injuries finally take their toll. The best stunt drivers evolve into stunt coordinators, designing the choreography of the stunts in consultation with the director, selecting the stunt performers, and making sure the stunts go off safely and acceptably. Of course, there are even fewer stunt coordinator positions than there are stunt drivers. In most cases, you need a broader background in all manner of stunts, not just driving. Short careers, however, also mean that there is high turnover. In addition, with the entertainment boom, opportunities will not be in short supply. It is important to become known as one of the best because directors and producers will always hire professionals with whom they've had success in the past.

FOR MORE INFORMATION

ASSOCIATIONS

Screen Actors Guild
5757 Wilshire Boulevard
Los Angeles, CA 90036-3600
(323) 954-1600
Web site: http://www.sag.org
The union for screen performers, which enforces fair working conditions and compensation. Their Web site provides information about joining whether you're a driver, stuntperson, or performer.

Stuntmen's Association of Motion Pictures
10660 Riverside Drive, 2nd Floor, Suite E
Toluca Lake, CA 91602
(818) 766 4334
Web site: http://www.stuntmen.com
A fraternal organization for professional stuntmen.

Stunts Canada
Web site: http://www.stuntscanada.net
The oldest association for Canadian stunt performers, based in Vancouver, British Columbia.

Stuntwomen's Association of Motion Pictures
Web site: http://home.earthlink.net/~stuntwomen
This association sets standards in medical benefits, wages, and compensation for female stunt professionals. It also provides networking opportunities and posts head shots and résumés of members.

WEB SITES

Bobby Ore School
http://www.bobbyoresports.com
Information on the school and stunt driving as a career.

BOOKS

Freese, Gene Scott. *Hollywood Stunt Performers: A Dictionary and Filmography of over 600 Men and Women, 1922–1996.* Jefferson, NC: McFarland & Company, 1998.
A survey of those who performed the deeds that thrilled audiences around the world. Short biographies and credits.

Ireland, Karin. *Hollywood Stuntpeople.* New York: Julian Messner, 1980.
A look at stunt performers and their work in film and television.

FOR FUN

The Fast and the Furious, 2001, available from Universal Home Video.
An undercover cop enters the world of street racers suspected of dealing in stolen goods. High octane adventure with great stunt work.

The French Connection, 1972, available from 20th Century-Fox Home Video.
Based on the real-life exploits of a detective nicknamed Popeye, Gene Hackman stars in this thriller. It has what many consider to be the greatest movie car chase ever, all handled by a stunt driver.

Gone in Sixty Seconds, 2000, available on video from Paramount Home Video.
Nicolas Cage stars in this movie about a group of car thieves who try to steal sixty cars in a single evening. Great stunt driving throughout.

The Stuntman, 1980, available on video from Anchor Bay.
Strong film with Peter O'Toole about the art and artifice of filmmaking.

7

TRUCK DRIVER

You see them everywhere. Eighteen-wheelers crowd the highways at all hours, they come rumbling through your neighborhood, and they have a mystique about them that has given rise to legends. The long-haul trucker has a solitary life, spending more time on the road than at home. It is isolated work with few interactions with others, except for the fraternity of other long-haul drivers at truck stops and weigh stations.

With 70 percent of all goods delivered by truck in North America, this is an extremely vital profession. Over three million people earn their living as truck drivers, according to 2000 government statistics, with another 209,000 drivers recorded in Canada in 1997. (Did you know that a truck crosses the United States–Canada border every three seconds?) Over 90 percent of truck drivers work for companies, and some 32 percent of those companies are involved in moving goods to wholesale and retail outlets. The remaining drivers work in other fields, such as construction and manufacturing.

To be considered a long-haul trucker, your vehicle has to be 26,000 gross vehicle weight. The size goes up from there, and each size has its own design and safety features.

Advancement in this profession occurs gradually. You may start out driving smaller trucks or work as a substitute driver before receiving your first long-distance run. With experience comes regular work and then more prestigious trucks or routes. Your compensation goes up accordingly. A handful of drivers will shift from behind the wheel to behind a desk, working for the company as a dispatcher or trip planner. Others leave for entirely different careers. Elvis Presley started driving a truck before leaving to become a musician.

Truck drivers are usually members of the International Brotherhood of Teamsters. This union helps negotiate the best possible wages and benefits for drivers and looks after issues of driver and vehicle safety. There are some specialized fields that require drivers to belong to those related unions instead of the Teamsters.

A typical driver will report to a terminal or warehouse (also known as a distribution center). He or she will inspect the vehicle, making sure it is in good working order and has fresh oil and gas. Brakes, horn, windshield wiper blades, and all the working parts are checked because the driver has to depend upon the vehicle for the duration of the trip. He or she then checks for supplies such as first aid, flares, fire extinguisher, and basic maintenance tools. (As a courtesy to all drivers, given that long-haul truckers ride higher than most other vehicles, if they see a traffic problem, they are the ones to alert authorities.)

The driver then makes sure that the cargo has been properly loaded and secured. In some instances, drivers will help do the loading and unloading. Not only does it get the job done quicker, but the driver is assured of a properly packed vehicle. Shifting boxes could cause the truck to lose its balance or the material could be damaged. Once on the road, the driver follows a route, so it's important to be familiar with the roads. Many drivers prefer a handful of

A truck driver uses a torch as he works on the drive shaft of his truck. Most truck drivers perform some level of maintenance on their vehicles.

A pair of truck drivers secure chains around a cargo of pipes for their trip. Drivers sometimes help to load cargo to make sure that the truck is properly packed.

regular routes because they know how to get around traffic problems rather than flounder around in unfamiliar territory. Others like to get out and see the country and take a different route every time, if they're not required to take the quickest route.

Given the duration of the trip, some drivers work in tandem with a partner. Some trucks have a space in the back of the cab where the second driver can sleep or rest while the other one drives. More often, though, the driver is alone.

When he or she reaches the destination, which may be another warehouse or a retail store, the driver makes sure everything is properly unloaded and signed for. At that point, federal regulations call for the driver to fill out a report detailing the trip and noting any problems that occurred along the way.

Being a truck driver is long, grueling work. To avoid routine traffic, truck drivers tend to attack the longest portions of their route during the night, on weekends, and even during holidays. Despite improvements in truck design over the years, drivers still feel fatigue from the hours of constantly being alert and handling such a powerful vehicle. They are aided with ergonomic seating, and newer model trucks now have global positioning systems (GPS) installed, which means they can get updated, computerized map information in case of an unforeseen detour or traffic problem. The GPS systems also mean a better stream of communication between the trucker and his company, which alleviates some of the tedium. The company, in turn, has a better sense of where the truck is according to the schedule, how the vehicle is performing, and other vital pieces of information.

Drivers also contend now with computerized inventory tracking systems, which means a little extra work at the loading and unloading points. The customer and the trucking company need to know not only where the truck is but also where the cargo is, especially if the truck is making multiple deliveries. The equipment is similar to the scanning devices employed by overnight delivery services. The computer scans in the bar code and matches it against the order for that particular load. In trucks using refrigerator equipment, they have even developed voice recognition programs to improve efficiency.

A driver's day and week are governed by regulations as determined by the state and federal governments. For example, a driver may not work more than sixty hours during a seven-day period. Also, after every ten hours of driving, the driver must have eight hours off. Drivers are happy to be looked after but most push the limit of the laws in order to make schedules or log additional miles for higher pay.

There is a great deal of satisfaction derived from a job well done, and many truck drivers enjoy the work. Before pursuing this, though, you may want to think about whether or not being away from home, family, and friends is something that might bother you.

A truck driver sits on a small bed in the cab of his truck after a nap. Because they often pass long hours on the road, truck drivers need to make sure they get enough rest.

Requirements

Trucking is a difficult profession that requires skills and attitudes beyond driving. You need a clean driving record and will need to obtain a CDL. Within your home state, you may be eighteen years old, but once you cross state lines, you are subject to federal regulations that mandate you being twenty-one years old. Typically, trucking firms look for drivers who are at least twenty-two.

Some states require a minimum level of truck driving school experience before issuing a license. Maine, for example, calls for an eight-hour course. There are many trucking schools around America to teach you all you'll need to know. The schools include classroom instruction that will help you with the written portion of the CDL exam. You will learn how to inspect your vehicle, how it operates, and how to drive safely before even putting the key in the ignition. Once you move the truck out of the parking lot, you will be taught how to maneuver on city streets and highways.

After obtaining your CDL and finding a job, your training will continue as the trucking company teaches you how to handle their vehicles and cargo. Companies look for drivers who will speak to people at both ends of the trip in a courteous manner. Your appearance should also be fairly neat and clean. Remember, you will be representing the company, so you need to make a good impression.

You may be asked to spend time with an experienced company driver before being given your first run.

Your company will routinely check your physical condition (while the government calls for every other year, most companies check their drivers annually) and will test you for drugs. Your physical condition calls for excellent eyesight and hearing in addition to free use of your arms and legs. People who are color-blind or suffer from epilepsy are not eligible for the CDL.

Salary

Because of the difficulty of the job and the lifestyle involved, truckers are well paid for their efforts. The median hourly income for heavy truck drivers was $15.25 in 2000. Long-haul truckers were generally better paid than trade contractors or construction workers. Those who transport beer, wine, and liquor are generally paid better than those hauling groceries.

Drivers tend to be paid by the hour or, for longer distances, by the mile. After the typical forty-hour week, drivers receive higher overtime pay. The size of the truck, your years of experience, and the cargo being carried all affect how much you will be paid. A commission is generally paid in addition to the hourly or per-mile wage. Those who are self-employed tend to bring home $20,000–25,000 a year after

A truck driver updates his logbook. It is important that truck drivers keep accurate records of their pickups and deliveries.

deductions are made for vehicle maintenance, insurance, and living expenses.

Outlook

In the coming decade, the job outlook for truck drivers is fairly positive. The U.S. government estimates that there should be enough turnover to present opportunities. This prediction is based on the cases of drivers retiring, leaving the field, or moving to the front office of a company.

FOR MORE INFORMATION

ASSOCIATIONS

American Trucking Associations, Inc.
2200 Mill Road
Alexandria, VA 22314
(703) 838-1700
Web site: http://www.truckline.com
A national organization that works to assure safe roads and laws that aid drivers.

Professional Truck Driver Institute
2200 Mill Road
Alexandria, VA 22314
(703) 838-8842
Web site: http://www.ptdi.org
This is a nonprofit organization to certify appropriate truck driving courses taught nationwide.

WEB SITES

Canada Trade
http://www.tradeport.org/ts/countries/canada/isa/isar0024.html
Offers an in-depth look at the trucking business in Canada, including job outlook and qualifications.

Monster.com
http://jobprofiles.monster.com
The truck driver profile offers a brief look at the career with links to related fields and current job opportunities.

Trucker Weather
http://www.truckerweather.com
A chance for truckers to check weather conditions along the route, with up to forty meteorologists on staff.

TruckingInfo.com
http://www.truckinginfo.com
A general purpose Web site with news, tips, and information for drivers.

Truckline
http://www.truckline.com/safetynet/drivers/careers.html
Offers a good look at the career paths in this field, including tips on looking for jobs and driving schools.

BOOKS

Byrnes, Mike, and associates. *Bumper to Bumper: The Complete Guide to Tractor-Trailer Operations,* 3rd edition. Tempe, AZ: Mike Byrnes & Assoc., 1997.
The nuts and bolts of how trucks work are explored in this book.

Professional Truck Drivers Institute. *Trucking: Tractor-Trailer Driver Handbook/Workbook*. Elk Grove, CA: Delmar Publishers. 1997.
A lot of the basics in handling a truck are covered in this volume.

Scharnberg, Ken. *Opportunities in Trucking Careers*. Chicago: VGM Career Horizons, 1999.
A good survey for those keenly interested in the field. The book covers careers, training, selecting a vehicle, and more.

Smith, John G. *Big Rigs*. New York: Book Sales, 1999.
A photographic look at the truck, critically acclaimed by those who drive them.

Woltman, Jeffrey, and Sheena Petitt Woltman. *Trucking Simplified (Tools and Strategies for Running a Successful Trucking Operation)*. Kapaa, HI: Boogaloo Press, 2000.
For those who want to start a company, large or small, this book offers strategies and tips.

PERIODICALS

Land Line Magazine
1 OOIDA Drive NW
Grain Valley, MO 64029
(800) 444-5791
Web site: http://www.landlinemag.com
A print and online magazine for all truck drivers.

Overdrive
(800) 633-5953
Web site: http://www.etrucker.com/default.asp?magid=1
For all truck drivers.

Today's Trucking
New Communications Group Inc.
130 Belfield Road
Etobicoke, ON M9W 1G1
Canada
(416) 614-2200
Web site: http://www.todaystrucking.com
A Canadian magazine for truck drivers. Available in print or online.

Truckers News
Web site: http://www.etrucker.com/default.asp?magid=2
This magazine is aimed at long-distance drivers. It also has an online version.

FOR FUN

Smokey and the Bandit, 1977, available from Universal Home Video. Burt Reynolds and Jerry Reed are hauling a load against an impossible deadline with Sheriff Jackie Gleason right behind them. This funny film typifies the fraternity of drivers on the highways.

RACE CAR DRIVER

Some people feel the need for speed. Some like the thrill of competition. Some just like driving something unique. If any of these things interest you, auto racing may be the profession for you. Auto racing is certainly not for everyone. Just getting into this particular occupation is not at all easy. First of all, it's a crowded field despite the many categories of racing (see page 84). Secondly, it takes a creative mind to figure out a way to earn a living doing this. There is a lot of competition in this field, especially with the increased interest in NASCAR racing around America.

It's also not a job that's easy to handle. Les Krantz's *Jobs Rated Almanac* places race car driver at number 248 (out of 250) for the worst working environment and number 246 for the most stress. You have to love car racing to pursue it.

A good racing school will help you develop leads to become a professional race car driver. Others will at least help point out directions. There are several race car organizations that sanction races and tracks, and by becoming affiliated with one or more, you can find out how to get hired. The oldest is the Sports Car Club of America (SCCA), and it runs its own schools in addition to sanctioning other institutions. A key difference between the schools is that the professional schools provide the cars and gear whereas the SCAA schools require you to provide your own (cars can be rented for such purposes).

Additionally, there is the National Auto Sport Association (NASA), formed in 1991, which promotes drag racing; the Midwestern Council of Sports Car Clubs, started in 1958 as a way to provide low-cost, low-pressure racing to drivers; and the International Conference of Sports Car Clubs, founded in 1957, dedicated to providing road racing in the Pacific Northwest.

Members of Winston Cup driver Sterling Marlin's pit crew scurry to work on his car as he makes a pit stop during the 2000 NASCAR UAW–DaimlerChrysler 400. Marlin won the race.

If you intend to drive, you need to put together a team. The team includes a head mechanic and pit crew, and the equipment involves the car, safety gear, tools to keep the car in shape, uniforms, and a driving outfit. This calls for a lot of money, and the only way to make a go of it is to use sponsors. All those logos you see on cars and uniforms advertising oil companies, car parts suppliers, and beer brands mean these businesses have invested a certain amount of money to sponsor the team. In turn, the driver is obligated to participate in a number of public races so the audience can see those logos and be reminded that those products exist.

Securing sponsorship is tricky, and there are books that can help you. A better way might be to start talking to the many professional drivers who teach at racing schools. Or go to races and start talking to the drivers and their crews.

As you gain experience and success on the track, you may be pleased to find that people seek you out. The best-known race car drivers in the world are sought out to drive cars sponsored by companies looking for a star behind the wheel. Those opportunities come rarely, and they come only to the best.

While waiting for that first job, you need to invest time and money in taking a car out onto a racetrack to get some practice. That's where schools and regional clubs can help. Many offer hourly access to tracks and cars.

With races large and small across the country every weekend of the year, in addition to auto shows and exhibitions, there is a reasonable amount of opportunity for the would-be racer. Unlike every other job described here, you must be dedicated to the physical and mental training required to handle a vehicle that can reach 250 mph in seconds. Sure, there's a thrill to feeling that speed, but it requires time, effort, and a lot of patience.

Race car driver Sarah Fisher poses for press cameras before taking her practice laps for the Indianapolis 500 at the Indianapolis Motor Speedway.

Requirements

If you want to be a race car driver, you need to have your driver's license and be eighteen. Then you will need to attend a specialized school. Since there are so many different styles of racing and race cars, you will have to do some homework and decide for yourself what appeals to you. After that, you will sign up for a training course. Once you pass, you will be eligible to take the required road test to get your license.

Many of the schools in America run two- or three-day courses. A typical three-day course covers the following schedule: Day one starts with thirty minutes of classroom instruction in safety. You will then spend an hour or so at a track, learning the operations of a race car. An instructor will walk the track with you, describing how to handle straightaways and turns. After the walk, you will drive the course in a normal car with the instructor. Finally, you will get behind the wheel of a special race car fitted with two seats. The instructor will accompany you. You'll drive a handful of laps to get a feel for the difference between a "street" car and a race car. After lunch, you return to the track, this time to drive several sets of laps on your own. Based on your skill, you will be encouraged to increase your speed.

Day two will begin with a set of laps to refresh yourself with the previous day's lessons. The morning will then be

How many kinds of race cars are there?

Most people are familiar with NASCAR's Formula One racers and drivers like Jeff Gordon and the Earnhardt family. These are the vehicles that look like sporty versions of "street" cars, and the races are usually televised, such as the Winston Cup. These cars are also known as stock cars.

Either the Championship Auto Racing Team or the Indy Racing League sanctions Indy cars. A key difference between the organizations is that the former has routes that mix track, ovals, and street routes, while the latter is strictly dedicated to oval courses. An Indy car is an open-wheel vehicle, meaning the wheels are in plain sight, not seen within a wheel well as in street cars. CART offers Indy Lights, aimed at younger racers.

Sprint cars are also open-wheeled vehicles but might be seen with large wings on either side, behind the driver. Sprint cars race on oval tracks in races like the World of Outlaws. Some sponsoring organizations prefer wingless cars and you need to do your homework before competing.

"Funny cars" are used mainly in exhibition auto shows and are not meant to be seen as anything other than entertaining. The same with monster trucks, which are normal flatbed truck chassis atop wheels that can be seven feet high. Monster trucks are also sponsored by corporations for publicity at auto shows, where these vehicles are seen crushing normal cars.

spent on working in teams to practice passing drills. After lunch, you spend the afternoon working on passing skills.

The third and final day begins with the morning in the garage, where a mechanic will instruct you on maintaining the race car. You need to learn what works on different types of tracks and with different cars. After lunch, you will run a final set of laps, this time simulating a race. You might be in a pack of four cars with the instructor in the lead position. The day ends with a graduation ceremony, certifying that you have passed the course.

What follows next is up to the driver.

Salary

"There is no single model race car driver," Rick Robins of JobsInMotorsports.com says. "Income can range from having to pay for your ride to the top F1 drivers making tens of millions of

Race car drivers competing in the Belgian Formula One Grand Prix. Race car driving is exciting, and the best drivers become celebrities. But it is also dangerous and stressful.

dollars per year not counting endorsements. Some careers peter out in a few years, but there is always Dick Trickle, who is still driving at 70 in NASCAR Winston Cup."

Outlook

Earning a living racing cars is a long shot, there's no doubt about it. But with hard work, experience, a lot of talent, and a bit of luck, it's possible to succeed.

FOR MORE INFORMATION

ASSOCIATIONS

International Conference of Sports Car Clubs
Web site: http://www.icscc.com
This loose confederation of independent clubs has no central office. You're directed to begin at their Web site to seek help within the organization.

Midwestern Council of Sports Car Clubs
3618 East 1769th Road
West Ottawa, IL 61350
(815) 434-9999
Web site: http://www.execpc.com/~mcscc
A grouping of sports car clubs, this council sponsors racing events.

NASCAR
P.O. Box 2875
Daytona Beach, FL 32120
(386) 253-0611
Web site: http://www.nascar.com
The best known of the racing organizations has information on sanctioned races, features profiles of drivers, and offers merchandise.

National Auto Sport Association
P.O. Box 21555
Richmond, CA 94820
(510) 232-6272
Web site: http://www.nasaproracing.com
This organization promotes races to professional and amateur drivers.

Sports Car Club of America (SCCA)
9033 East Easter Place
Centennial, CO 80112
(800) 770-2055
Web site: http://www.scca.org
According to its Web site, the SCCA "is a 65,000-member nonprofit organization featuring the most active membership participation organization in motor sports today, with over 2,000 amateur and professional motor sports events each year."

WEB SITES

About.com Auto Racing Schools
http://autoracing.about.com/cs/schools
A good source for listings of driving schools.

JobsinMotorSports.com
http://www.jobsinmotorsports.com
A relatively new site designed to match up employers and employees, complete with links and other useful information.

Motorsports.com
http://www.na-motorsports.com/Schools/#Racing
Provides more in-depth information on the various kinds of driving schools and race organizations operating today.

BOOKS

Burt, Bill. *Stock Car Race Shop: Design and Construction of a NASCAR Stock Car*. Osceola, WI: MotorBooks International, 2001.
It's one thing to know how to drive it, but it's just as important to understand how stock cars are built to handle the speed and pressures of racing.

Jackson, Terry. *Anatomy of Speed: Inside the World's Great Race Cars*. New York: Book Sales, 1996.
A look at the different manufacturing methods in making winning race cars.

Lord, Trevor. *Big Book of Race Cars*. New York: DK Publishing, 2001.
A graphic representation of how these cars work. An excellent beginner's guide.

PERIODICALS

Auto Racing Digest.
Century Publishing Company
Dept. WEB01
990 Grove Street
Evanston, IL 60201-4370
Web site: http://www.centurysports.net/autoracing
This is a good introduction to the racing world. It covers auto racing including NASCAR, CART, and IRL, as well as the Formula One Grand Prix circuit in Europe and Asia.

Hot Rod
Web site: http://www.hotrod.com
A well-established magazine designed for the fan.

Popular Hot Rodding
Corporate Headquarters
McMullen Argus Publishing Inc.
2400 East Katella Avenue, 11th Floor
Anaheim, CA 92806
(714) 939-2400
Web site: http://www.popularhotrodding.com
The emphasis here is on performance, bolt-on accessories, replacement parts, safety, and the sport of drag racing.

Stock Car Racing
Web site: http://www.stockcarracing.com
This magazine's features include technical articles, profiles of standouts in the field, and reports on the most important racetracks, series, and events.

FOR FUN

Days of Thunder, 1990, available from Paramount Home Video.
Tom Cruise is a race car driver competing in the toughest race of his life.

Grand Prix, 1966, available from Warner Home Video.
Amiable James Garner is an American competing in France's famous Grand Prix.

MOVER

When a family needs to move to a new house or town, they usually hire a professional moving company to handle their possessions. Moving companies employ people who drive their trucks and help with the move.

After long-distance hauling, the mover is the next most common profession for a truck driver. In fact, people in this job are a mix of driver and mover. They log nowhere near as many miles as other drivers.

Of the many professions described in this book, you should note that movers enjoy the most varied set of personal contacts and locations. If you like people and working in a team environment, this may be the career for you. Many movers tend to be young people working their way through college, newlyweds, or retired service people.

For families, summer is the most common time to relocate because school is out and it's easiest on the children. For businesses, moves tend to happen throughout the rest of the year, when school is in session and the rates are lower at many moving companies, given the slow business.

Movers get training, not only in the type of vehicles a particular company uses but in the actual moving process itself. Your company will show you how to help load delicate and heavy objects, how to protect them from getting damaged, and how to maneuver them through tricky corners and doorways. Many moving companies offer packing services, and the team that performs the move normally does this job as well. This gives the movers a better idea of what is being moved and what to be careful with, and assures them that everything has been safely packed for the move.

Having access to someone's home and belongings requires a certain degree of trust. You need to maintain that trust by treating the customers' objects with respect in

A mover carries chairs to be loaded onto the moving van. Movers need to take great care when handling their clients' belongings.

addition to answering questions from the nervous family preparing to relocate.

There are many nationwide moving companies that handle everything from commercial to residential moves. They have specialty divisions that handle different kinds of businesses, from high-tech to refrigerated operations. These companies will offer the required training to make sure you know how to properly do your job. Regional and independent moving companies will handle one or a few kinds of moves, perhaps specializing in a particular niche part of the market. Most of these handle residential moves.

There are many independent truck owners who run their own small moving businesses or contract their services to other local companies that need help. Owner-operators can make a great deal of money compared to hourly wages offered to drivers at larger companies, since they get to set their rates. Their overhead is minimal, beyond caring for the truck and moving equipment. Their biggest additional expense is hiring local day laborers to help with a specific assignment.

Another option is to maintain good relationships with other movers. As with long-haul truck drivers, there is a fraternal feel between movers. Many times, these drivers will help one another with loading or unloading rather than contract other helpers. In this case, tradition calls for the help to be treated to a nice dinner, which is substantially cheaper than hiring local laborers.

The length of each assignment will depend upon the items to be moved, whether they need to be packed, and how far away the destination is. At minimum, a move can be done in a day, but most are several days long. Drivers and other workers will arrive at the home on moving day and wrap furniture in quilted moving blankets, carefully carrying or wheeling them from the house to the truck. Loading the truck can almost be an art form, given the need to fit everything in and secure it so the load will not shift during the drive, which could potentially cause the truck to lose balance. This will take part or all of a day.

Once the driver reaches the destination, the family will direct the moving team where everything should go. Furniture is placed at the owner's discretion, and the crew has to have patience when things don't quite fit as expected.

Some companies run huge trucks (typically nine feet wide and thirteen feet tall) that can be filled with two or more households' belongings. These are for the longer distance moves, such as from coast to coast. In this case, a driver will take the truck from house to house, supervising the loading of each house with local labor. Then, the long drive begins, making the required stops along the way until the first household loaded is the last household unloaded. While this means families wait weeks for their belongings to arrive, the cost savings is more often than not worth the time. For the driver, it could mean being on the road for weeks at a time. If you like seeing America, this has its appeal.

Paperwork is absolutely necessary in this business since you need to document what has been loaded, what wear and tear has been noted on furniture and other belongings, and when you left the first destination. This protects you, the family, and the company you work for. You then need to review all the paperwork at the destination, again confirming that everything has been delivered and is in good shape. Insurance companies demand strict

recording procedures, which companies strive to accommodate. It's in everyone's best interests to handle this with care, and the driver, as team leader, has to be comfortable with this aspect of the job.

It should be noted that a related business is driving cars from destination to destination for people. Usually this is because the customer is flying to a new home or has bought a car far from home and needs it to be brought to them. Individuals, negotiating rates on a case-by-case basis, usually handle this service.

Requirements

If you want to explore this field, you need to make sure you not only have the physical requirements to pass the CDL exam but also a strong back, arms, and legs. Additionally, you need patience and the ability to work with all types of personalities. You are, after all, being put in charge of someone's belongings. Customer service is a key requirement in this kind of position.

Salary

Movers don't get paid by the hour or by the mile. Instead, they receive a percentage of the "line haul," a percentage of the fee earned by the moving company. Owner-operators of moving

Moving company workers load a moving van. Movers need to be physically fit because their work involves a lot of heavy lifting.

vehicles can contract with a company for an even higher fee. Being away from home can actually provide you with substantial income, since you will be paid lodging and other expenses.

Outlook

Becoming a mover is one of the easier professions to enter because there are so many companies around the nation. Additionally, because of the extra training required, this seems to scare off some drivers. There is also a high amount of turnover as people stop moving to return to school or change careers. There will be no shortage of opportunities in this field.

FOR MORE INFORMATION

ASSOCIATIONS

American Moving and Storage Association (AMSA)
1611 Duke Street
Alexandria, VA 22314
(703) 683-7410
Web site: http://www.moving.org
AMSA is organized to help the consumer, but check out their Web site for information about the more than 3,200 professional moving companies that are members.

American Trucking Associations, Inc.
2200 Mill Road
Alexandria, VA 22314
(703) 838-1700
Web site: http://www.truckline.com
This is a nonprofit organization that looks after the needs of truck drivers.

Canadian Association of Movers
590 Alden Road, Suite 211
Markham, ON L3R 892
Canada
(905) 513-1728
Web site: http://www.mover.net
Professional association for movers in Canada.

Professional Truck Driver Institute
2200 Mill Road
Alexandria, VA 22314
(703) 838-8842
Web site: http://www.ptdi.org
This is a nonprofit organization to certify appropriate truck driving courses taught nationwide.

WEB SITES

Glossary of Moving Terms
http://www.bankrate.com/latc/news/moving_on/Edit/movedef.asp
This Web site has a useful glossary of terms unique to the moving business.

Monster.com
http://jobprofiles.monster.com
The truck driver profile offers a brief look at the career with links to related fields and current job opportunities.

Trucker Weather

http://www.truckerweather.com

A chance for truckers to check weather conditions along the route, with up to forty meteorologists on staff.

TruckingInfo.com

http://www.truckinginfo.com

A general purpose Web site with news, tips, and information for drivers.

Truckline

http://www.truckline.com/safetynet/drivers/careers.html

Offers a good look at the career paths in this field, including tips on looking for jobs and driving schools.

10

POSTAL WORKER

Everyone knows their motto: "Neither snow nor rain nor heat nor gloom of night stays these couriers from the swift completion of their appointed rounds." But does everyone understand what it takes to actually live up to those words? Six days a week, mail is delivered to most people in America by thousands of workers.

Some of the country's mail is delivered by postal carriers who travel on foot. But in other areas, mail routes are not possible to walk. Those carriers drive from house to house and building to building. Some carriers drive mail trucks, but in rural areas, some carriers use their own cars. In addition to the carriers who have their own daily route, the U.S. Postal Service needs drivers to truck the mail from city to city.

There is a high demand for positions within the post office, in large part due to job security and terrific benefits. In 1998, there were 332,000 carriers with all but 5 percent being full-time employees. Those not full-time might be considered casual (ninety-day hires for peak periods such as Christmas). Part-timers are called in as needed. Part-timers regularly fill in for sick or vacationing carriers. If you are accepted into the service, you can expect to start in one of these positions.

There is normally a one- to two-year wait for an opening, which means most people take other jobs while waiting for an opportunity. For example, while waiting, you might want to become a local deliveryperson, learning the local area routes, which will give you experience for when the opportunity presents itself.

Once hired, you will be sent to a regional center for training. Currently, this training takes three days and covers

A postman delivers mail to roadside mailboxes. Few people know a neighborhood better than the postal carrier who works that route.

the operation of mail trucks, sorting mail, learning the routes, and the safety techniques you must master. After that, you are assigned to a post office where you will continue your training. As new technologies get introduced, such as the recent bar code scanners for Express Mail, additional training will be provided.

After that, you are assigned a route and given your first stack of mail to finish sorting and then deliver. When you hit the streets, you must remember that you are a representative of the postal service. This means putting on a friendly face despite complaints from people about too much mail, too little mail, the wrong mail, misdelivered mail, late mail, and many other problems. Frequently, motorists will stop you to ask for directions. As a representative of the postal service, you must always be polite, friendly, and helpful.

Most carriers start their day early, in some cases before the sun rises. As a postal carrier, you arrive at the post office and complete the sorting of mail for your route. You then load your pouches and vehicle and head out to begin your rounds. Once away from the building, you are pretty much left on your own to complete the route. This gives many mail carriers a sense of independence. Of course, the work is performed no matter how bad the weather may be. You will have rain gear plus hats and mittens for inclement weather.

Once the route is complete, you return to the post office to drop off your gear. You might file reports of problems, such as something hazardous on the route that may need a town's attention, or a note warning potential replacement carriers of a vicious dog on the route.

For those interested, carriers can advance into management roles within the postal system as opportunity and performance warrants. In the meantime, with seniority comes the ability to select preferable routes or hours.

A postal worker sorts packages for delivery in the back of his truck.

Requirements

For those interested in handling the trucks, the same training is required as with long-haul truckers and movers. To be a carrier, you must be at least eighteen years old and a U.S. citizen or be a permanent resident-alien. You must pass a written test to prove you can read addresses, sort mail, and learn routes and related areas. Applicants are also required to pass a physical exam and drug test. You need to demonstrate the ability to lift, without strain, mail sacks weighing a maximum of seventy pounds. Candidates will additionally need to possess a driver's license and a clean driving record, and they may be asked to take a road test.

The written tests are given on a regular basis, and you should check with your local post offices to find when they will next be given in your area. Should you pass the test, you will be listed in order of grade. When an opening occurs, the local postmaster will contact people on the list from the top scorers on down. Your scores remain good for two years, at which time you will be required to retake the test.

Salary

Full-time mail carriers earn a median salary of $34,840, according to 1998 statistics. As of March 2001, new carriers start at $15.30 per hour. After twelve and a half years, a top carrier stands to earn $20.34 per hour. In addition, carriers

A rural mail carrier empties mail from a box on the side of a road. Rural carriers generally cover a wider area than do postal workers in heavily populated urban centers.

receive a complete benefits package that includes medical coverage, sick days, vacation days, and a retirement plan. Workers are generally members of either the American Postal Workers Union or the National Association of Letter Carriers, both of which are affiliated with the American Federation of Labor–Congress of Industrial Organizations (AFL-CIO).

Outlook

It is anticipated that openings in the post office will be fewer than in many other industries covered in this book through

2008. However, within the postal service, mail carriers will experience the greatest growth potential. As automated "delivery point sequencing" systems improve, there will be less time required for the carriers to sort the mail themselves. This may mean that carriers will be given longer routes to utilize the extra time they'll have. In turn, this could result in fewer job openings for carriers. As technology and the economy progress, these situations may become clearer.

Profile

Valerie Jacob is a fifteen-year veteran of the United States Postal Service, working the same route in Connecticut for the last nine years. She enjoys her job, and she can happily recall the weekend she began her current route in 1993.

WHAT DO YOU NEED TO DRIVE A MAIL VAN?

Just your driver's license and a clean record.

HOW DID YOU LEARN?

I went to vehicle training with an instructor. It used to be we had a few days of training up in New Haven with a lot of safety training. These days they run a Carrier Academy for three weeks and they drill you on all facets of the job, including driving.

WHAT'S IT LIKE DRIVING THE VEHICLE?

It's all mirrors and no rear or side windows, so it's a little awkward. You also drive on the right side so you can exit close to the house or mailbox and not on the street.

WHAT'S GOOD ABOUT YOUR JOB?

The independence. I'm in charge of my work even though there's still supervision from the branch. I enjoy talking to people, so the social element is good. There's room for different personalities, so if you're antisocial, you can get routes where you don't interact with a lot of people.

WHAT'S NOT SO GOOD?

Some of the dogs. The weather is a challenge. Ice is the worst: the slips and falls, twisted ankles, and the like. We can fill out warning cards for substitute or replacement carriers so they know where the problem spots are.

FOR MORE INFORMATION

ASSOCIATIONS

American Postal Workers Union
1300 L Street NW
Washington, DC 20005
(202) 842-4200 or (202) 842-8500
Web site: http://www.apwu.org
According to its Web site, "The American Postal Workers Union, AFL-CIO, represents 366,000 employees of the U.S. Postal Service who are

clerks, maintenance employees, motor vehicle operators, and non-mail-processing professional employees."

Canada Post
P.O. Box 1689 HFS Cent
Purdy's Tower II, 7th floor
Halifax, NS B3J 2B1
Canada
(800) 267-1177
Web site: http://www.canadapost.ca/segment-e.asp
Canada's postal service.

National Association of Letter Carriers, AFL-CIO
100 Indiana Avenue NW
Washington, DC 20001-2144
(202) 393-4695
Web site: http://www.nalc.org
Growing out of the Milwaukee Letter Carriers Association in the nineteenth century, this group is one of two main unions representing carriers' interests.

United States Postal Services
(800) ASK-USPS (275-8777)
Web site: http://www.usps.com
America's postal service. The Web site contains information regarding all of its services, allows you to order stamps, and provides information regarding employment opportunities.

BOOKS

Chiu, David. *Choosing a Career in the Post Office*. New York: The Rosen Publishing Group, Inc., 2001.
A good guide to the different job opportunities within the postal service.

Damp, Dennis V. *Post Office Jobs: How to Get a Job with the U.S. Postal Service,* 2nd edition. Moon Township, PA: Bookhaven Press, 2000.
A detailed look at what it takes to qualify for the different service positions.

Parnell, T. W., and Susie Varner. *Postal Exam Training Guide: General Entrance Test Battery 470 & Rural Carrier Exam 460, Free Live Support & Guaranteed Score of 95-100%*. Pinehurst, TX: Pathfinder Distributing Company, 2000.
As titled, a training guide to help score as high as possible on the postal test, enhancing your chances of being selected when an opportunity arises.

11

SANITATION WORKER

Refuse, sanitation, or garbage—call it what you will, collecting and removing it is a job that needs to be done in every North American town and city. Depending upon the town, the work is done either by a member of the public works department or by an independent company.

Like postal workers, sanitation workers perform their jobs in all

Sanitation workers carry trash from the sidewalk to the garbage truck. They wear protective gear to minimize the chances of being infected by the refuse they transport.

kinds of weather. They must be strong and fit and willing to do a lot of walking, hefting, and driving. They must also be willing to put up with waste. This means all forms of garbage, whether neatly placed in bags or loosely tossed in receptacles. If the garbage has been sitting for days, natural components have started decomposing, which produces unpleasant odors.

As a sanitation worker, you need to be polite to the customer who complains that you don't put the cans back in the right place or that you missed some of the garbage.

Others will ask you to pick up something you are not legally allowed to take, and you have to be firm but polite when you decline.

Driving a garbage route means a different set of neighborhoods every day, starting at an early hour and usually ending in the early afternoon. Most garbage pick up is done in the mornings, before school buses and morning commuters crowd the streets. Of course, this means you might be loud enough to wake people, especially in warmer weather when people tend to keep their windows open.

"If you're interested in what I do, just watch when the truck comes down your street. I love my job," Helen Milne told students at Canada's Turner Fenton Campus. "There is no stress. The garbage doesn't yell at you and that makes a difference. I used to work in an office and never thought I'd be doing this. It's not for everyone, but I enjoy it."

When drivers have completed their route, they report to a processing center where their trucks are unloaded. In Chicago, for example, the trucks are dropped off at the end of the day, and a second shift unloads them, processes the waste, then cleans and preps the trucks for the following morning. These collection points handle the garbage according to town and state guidelines, recycling what can be salvaged and handling the rest with the least harmful impact to the environment.

Drivers no longer just drive. These days the three-man crew has been gradually reduced to two-man or even one-man operations. Therefore, the driver not only needs to know how to operate and maintain a truck but must also be physically fit enough to lift heavy cans of refuse all day long. It has been estimated that garbage collectors walk some twenty miles (thirty-two kilometers) a day on a typical route.

It's important to note that there can be some danger involved in this job. Between 1980 and 1992, 450 garbage workers lost their lives in job-related accidents involving their trucks. Additionally, some have been injured or killed as a result of some of the refuse they handle. All municipalities have stringent requirements regarding what may or may not be collected by these operators, but some people flaunt the laws, and it's the men and women who remove the refuse who suffer. Over the last few years, a growing number of injuries were the result of improperly disposed medical waste, including used syringes. According to a 1995 report from the U.S. Bureau of Labor Statistics, there were 2,236 instances of lost workdays nationally because of injuries to garbage collectors working for private haulers. This figure

A sanitation worker empties a bin of recyclables. Like other garbage, these need to be handled carefully to avoid injuries from broken glass or sharp edges.

does not even include injuries or lost days for garbage collectors working for county and city collection services. Drivers and collectors have to be careful, even with bins full of recycled material. Glass can break, and plastic jugs can have sharp edges.

Today, modern technology has come into play to help garbage collectors perform their jobs more efficiently. Los Angeles, for example, has a massive new computer complex set up to monitor street and traffic conditions as well as construction projects. New routes can be mapped out for drivers so they can avoid becoming part of the typical Los Angeles traffic snarl. The garbage trucks are being outfitted with terminals, which will provide up-to-the-minute information and instructions.

Requirements

Towns that provide garbage collection services hire workers like they do for most other positions. The candidate must fill out an application, pass a physical, and endure a background check. To operate a garbage truck, you will need a CDL. The town will not train you for this test; you will have to possess a CDL when you apply for the job.

If you buy your own truck and become an independent contractor, there are many different vehicles to choose from. In just about every case, some manner of commercial

A sanitation worker uses a snowplow to clear snow from the streets. The work may not be glamorous, but it is one of the most valuable services in every community.

license will be required, and you will have to check with your town and state to find out the specific requirements.

Salary

For those working directly for the government, you have union-set wages, by the hour, complete with benefits that include medical, vacation time, sick days, and a retirement plan. You're likely to work a five-day week with the potential for overtime since public works staff gets pressed into duty during snowfalls. Garbage truck drivers can also double as snowplow or sanding truck drivers. Overtime is paid accordingly.

Other areas prefer to let private enterprises collect the trash, which drives companies to compete for the jobs. In some cases, there are unwritten agreements that divide a town, granting a virtual monopoly to some companies. Some states have started fighting this practice, since increased competition means better collection prices for residents. Private firms charge a monthly fee, collecting the trash once a week and recyclables on a different day. One-man operations usually cover an entire town that is ignored by the larger firms.

Private firms generally pay slightly better than the government pays, but the benefits are not as good. Before applying, check your area and see what the options are.

Outlook

Given the amount of waste generated by Americans every day, there will remain a strong need for garbage drivers and collectors in the years to come. In the book *One Hundred Jobs*, a sanitation worker told author Ron Howell, "This is the best job I've ever had with the city." The worker added that he knew he was in a good position when people in suits walked up and asked him how to apply for a job as trash collector.

Profile

Thomas H. Van Weelden, CEO, Allied Waste Industries in Scottsdale Arizona, the second largest waste management company in the United States.

"As a kid, I used to hear a lot of snide remarks about being the garbage man's son," Thomas H. Van Weelden wrote in Reader's Digest. *"But my hero wasn't the pitcher who could throw a 98-mile-an-hour fast ball—it was the garbage man who could handle two full 55-gallon steel drums at once." Van Weelden is president and CEO of Allied Waste Industries, and he began his career working for his father. "I started swabbing out trucks for Dad when I was fourteen. It was miserable, filthy work. I had to steam-clean every corner and dig out by hand every bit of trash, maggots and all."*

At sixteen Van Weelden started driving the trucks and collecting garbage. "I learned quickly that in the garbage business you are judged by your customers every day," he wrote. "You can service a client faithfully for five years, but miss just one pickup and you have wiped out all that hard-earned good will." During the school year he collected past-due bills, which taught him to handle difficult situations and to work with customers.

"The decisions I make today are no different from those I made nearly thirty years ago," he wrote. Customer service and quality of the job are key. All new operations managers in his company must have two years of experience driving trucks. That way they have more experience with which to direct the drivers.

FOR MORE INFORMATION

ASSOCIATIONS

The American Federation of Labor–Congress of Industrial Organizations (AFL-CIO)
815 16th Street NW
Washington, DC 20006
(202) 637-5000
Web site: http://www.AFL-CIO.org
According to its Web site, the AFL-CIO is "the voluntary federation of America's unions, representing more than 13 million working women and men nationwide."

WEB SITES

Custom Diecast Trucks
http://www.customdiecasttrucks.com
Custom diecast manufacturer offers ⅟₃₂, ⅟₃₄, and ⅟₅₀ scale truck replicas, featuring roll off container, flatbed tow trucks, flatbed with cranes, Autocar, Brockway, R-Mack, LJ-Mack, B-Mack, Peterbilt, and Kenworth.

BOOKS

Montville, John B. *Refuse Trucks: Photo Archive*. Hudson, MA: Iconografix, 2001.
A look at the different kinds of trucks used for garbage collection over the years.

Rathje, William, and Cullen Murphy. *Rubbish! The Archeology of Garbage.* New York: HarperCollins Publishers, 1992.
This book tells you everything you ever wanted to know about garbage.

Ross, Allison J., and Scott Harrison. *Choosing a Career in Waste Management.* New York: The Rosen Publishing Group, Inc., 2000.
This book discusses all aspects of the waste management industry, from recycling to hazardous waste.

12

TAXI DRIVER

The yellow cab is a part of American culture, and almost anyone can drive one for a living. Driving a cab is seen as either a lonely, miserable job or one that is exciting, since each fare is an opportunity to meet someone new. Cabs come in all sizes, shapes, and colors around America. For people who would like to make their living behind the wheel of a truck or car, driving a cab is perhaps the easiest way to start.

At the beginning of their shifts, cab drivers report to the cab company and inspect the vehicle they'll be using for the day. In most cases, they have a display with their hack's license and photo, intended to assure passengers that a licensed driver is behind the wheel. In suburban areas, many drivers wait at the company until a call comes. Some wait by train or bus stations, usually keeping copies of arrival schedules in the glove compartment.

Dispatchers, usually former drivers themselves, have to have an intimate knowledge of the geography of the region so that the cabs keep moving from one drop-off to another pickup. Coming back to the office means downtime and lost moneymaking opportunities.

In cities, drivers tend to cruise the streets, waiting to be flagged down by customers. Many drivers park at airports or hotels, lining up and waiting for an attendant/doorman to call them forward. There might be dispatcher calls as well, but most city drivers work independently and enjoy the freedom they get.

Requirements

You will need a driver's license and the special hack's license required for commercial driving. To get a hack's license,

you'll have to pass a written and driving test. You will need to know details on regulations affecting cab drivers. This is public information, available at libraries, town halls, or on the Internet.

Some companies will require up to eighty hours of training. You will need to demonstrate a thorough knowledge of a region and how to get to popular destinations such as train stations, landmarks, and theaters. You will also need to learn how to use the meter and two-way radio.

Cab drivers are subject to town, state, and federal regulations, so you need to check with your local cab company to see what requirements might exist beyond your license. Larger companies will check for criminal records in addition to medical and driving histories. Insurance regulations encourage companies to hire drivers a little older than high school age, which might mean as old as twenty-five.

As a cab driver, you need to be polite, able to understand directions, and able to answer questions. You need to be patient with all types of personalities, including backseat drivers who might dictate your route or critique your driving. Patience will be required to deal with those

A commuter hails a taxi at a busy city intersection. Working as a taxi driver brings one into contact with people from all walks of life.

passengers who have had too much to drink and are being ferried home for their safety, or boisterous students who think the party is still continuing. It is important to remember that you will be representing the company, and if you anger a customer, he or she may refuse to use the company in the future.

Similarly, you need patience to handle heavy traffic, especially in a city or where highway driving is required. If you get angry, it might cause you physical distress or upset the passenger.

Larger companies tend to offer on-the-job training, making sure the driver really can get from point A to point B in the most efficient manner. In the majority of cases, cab companies have set rates that start with a high number for the first mile and then a set price for each division of a mile. In New York City, for example, it's $2 for the first mile and 30¢ for each additional fifth of a mile. Other municipalities have regional rates.

You're shown how to use the taximeter and radio, plus what to look for in terms of vehicle maintenance. If you drive the same car for eight or ten hours at a time, you will

Taxi drivers find fares at airports and tend to meet people from around the world.

A driver collects a fare from a rider. Tips make up a significant portion of a taxi driver's income.

be the one to notice mechanical problems. Drivers are the ones who gas up the vehicle and usually clean it out at the end of a shift.

In many cases, drivers lease a vehicle from a company or have their own car and affiliate themselves with a cab company. This involves a fee paid from the driver to the company for the customers assigned, but the driver tends to keep more of the money. If you have your own vehicle, though, you will be the one required to keep the car in good condition in addition to paying the insurance premium.

For those operating on their own, you should note that many cities limit the number of vehicles that can operate as taxis. In New York City, that's controlled through the assignment of "medallions," which can be seen on the hood of all properly registered vehicles. This limits the competition and the number of vehicles crowding the streets. In San Francisco, for example, there are thirty-three companies sanctioned to operate taxicabs.

Salary

The median wage for a salaried cabbie in 2000 was $8.19 an hour. Depending upon the hours worked and tips earned, a driver could do significantly better than it first appears. Some drivers receive extra money for driving the night shift, and some cities, such as New York, add a surcharge for trips taken after a certain time. City drivers tend to get higher hourly wages than suburban drivers, but it's harder to say which region tips better. It's estimated that the majority of drivers earn between $18,000 and $21,000 per year. Those who own and drive their own vehicle can make upwards of $30,000.

Outlook

In 2000, some 59,000 people drove a cab. According to the Department of Labor, the job outlook looks strong through

2010 given the high rate of turnover across the country. Many cab companies add to their staff during peak seasons such as the holidays, which lead to full-time positions. Cab drivers often move on to related work, like driving a truck or limousine, or they may change their profession entirely. There are few who drive a cab their entire lives. In Les Krantz's *Jobs Rated Almanac*, driving a cab rated 246 out of 250 careers in terms of work conditions and stress.

Profile

Dave Thibodeaux has been driving a taxi for the Fairfield Taxi Company in Fairfield, Connecticut, for the last twelve years.

HOW DID YOU GET STARTED?

After high school, I was a mechanic for ten years, and I had friends who worked at the cab company. I started driving part-time, on Sundays, for a few extra bucks. I went full-time when I couldn't stand my job anymore. One year turned into twelve and here I am.

WHAT DO YOU LIKE ABOUT THE JOB?

It's never the same thing. You're not stuck in an office and you get out and about. It's different every day. You get to flirt and mingle. Since I'm a people person, this is great.

DID IT TAKE LONG TO LEARN YOUR WAY AROUND?

I grew up here and pretty much knew my way around. I've helped guys who grew up out of town learn.

WHAT ARE THE BEST KIND OF PASSENGERS?

The ones who tip well, of course! Everyone looks forward to the big job, something like ten miles plus.

WHAT ARE THE WORST KIND OF PASSENGERS?

Drunks. They're mostly students from the university, but we get our share from the bars. They're only bad because some get belligerent, and some get sick in the cab. And the ones with baskets full of groceries.

I've only had about two fares not pay in my twelve years so that's not a problem. You get stiffed—no one at the pickup—about once a day.

WHAT ABOUT THE BACK-SEAT DRIVERS?

They're fine. I'll follow any route they give because usually it's the longer way, which adds to the fare and tip.

A taxi driver gives directions to a passenger after letting him off on a busy street.

DO YOU GET A LOT OF REGULARS?

Lots of regulars. You can develop relationships with some of the regulars you meet. There's a definite advantage to driving since you meet so many people. I know drivers who married people they met while driving.

WHAT'S YOUR DAY LIKE?

I have pretty much worked the same shift since I started. I start around 4 AM and drive until 2 or 4 in the afternoon. I check my car and then start driving. I'll do between twenty to twenty-five trips per shift, and I work a five-day week. At the end of the shift I'll gas up so the car is full for the next driver. Sometimes I'll dispatch.

WHAT'S THAT LIKE?

It's like being an air traffic controller or playing chess. You have to keep a map of the town in your mind and keep everyone—we have ten cars—moving. I don't prefer it. It's a much more stressful job.

IS DRIVING DANGEROUS?

Around here it's not as dangerous as a big city. All of the fares call us for rides, we don't pick up hails. You know who you're picking up that way.

You do get to be the eyes and ears of the police department. They'll ask us to look for suspects and give us a physical description. I recently picked up a guy at motel who just robbed a store in Westport and had him picked up. We've nabbed a few guys and that's fun.

FOR MORE INFORMATION

ASSOCIATIONS

Taxi drivers may belong to local unions, which act on their behalf. There is no national organization for this profession.

WEB SITES

Taxis Around the World

http://www.taxi-L.org

A site dedicated to images and discussion regarding cabs and their drivers.

Taxi 2000

http://www.taxi2000.com

A Web site devoted to showcasing the development of the next generation of taxicabs and their dispatching systems.

The Ultimate Taxi

http://www.ultimatetaxi.com

A site complete with Web cameras and photos of celebrities driver Jon Barnes has driven in Aspen, Colorado.

BOOKS

Frolov, Andrei. *The Stories of a Taxi Driver.* New York: Vantage Press, 1994. You meet all sorts of people when driving a cab, and this veteran talks about the memorable ones.

Johnson, John. *Taxi! True Stories from Behind the Wheel.* Toronto: Macmillan of Canada, 2001. A look at the different people aboard a Canadian cab.

Mosher, Tim, and Stuart Allen Taub. *New York City Taxi & Limousine Drivers Guide*. Maspeth, NY: Hagstrom Map Co., 1988.
Tips for getting around New York City's five boroughs, possibly the trickiest region in America for a cabbie.

FOR FUN

Gridlock
http://www.geocities.com/gridlock_cartoon
A Web-based comic strip about the drivers for a cab company.

GLOSSARY

commercial driver's license A special license that enables the bearer to drive buses and trucks.

dispatcher A person who sends cabs, limousines, and trucks on their routes, and also tracks where all the vehicles are and who should be assigned to the next available job.

gross vehicle weight A federal weight measuring the motorcoach or truck while empty. Anything over 26,000 GVW is considered a truck and is subject to Department of Transportation guidelines, which may mean limits as to which roads can be used.

hack's license A commercial driver's license that enables people to operate limousines and taxicabs.

long haul A term denoting the distance traveled, usually by a contracted motorcoach, truck, or moving vehicle. This tends to mean in excess of a few hundred miles but does not have a specific cut-off point.

median wage A term meaning that there are as many salary levels above a certain point as there are below it.

meter Taxicabs, buses, and limousines tend to use some form of meter to track distances traveled and monies owed.

motorcoach A large vehicle used for transporting students, such as a school bus, or passengers, such as a city bus.

subcontractor A person who owns his or her own vehicle and/or business and is then hired by a larger operation to perform services on their behalf.

INDEX

About the Author

Robert Greenberger has written about a diverse range of nonfiction subjects and has written fiction usually featuring characters from *Star Trek*. He also has published several original short stories. His articles have covered celebrity interviews to historic essays. His great passion is baseball. As a publishing executive, he has logged many years at DC Comics and Marvel Comics. He makes his home in Connecticut with his wife, Deb, and children, Katie and Robbie. He proudly drives a 1995 Saturn SL-2.

Photo Credits

Design and Layout

Evelyn Horovicz